D1717054

From a Super Continent to Seven

The Pangaea and the Continental Drift

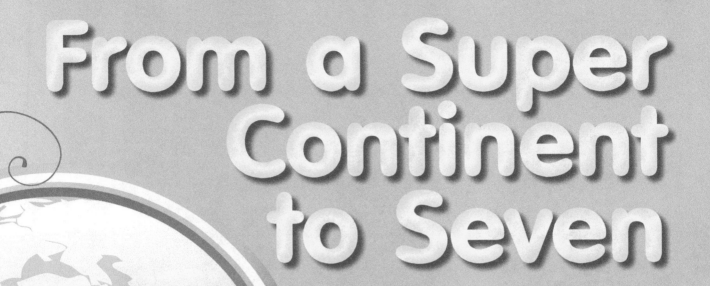

Grade 5 | Children's Earth Sciences Books

First Edition, 2020

Published in the United States by Speedy Publishing LLC, 40 E Main Street, Newark, Delaware 19711 USA.

© 2020 Baby Professor Books, an imprint of Speedy Publishing LLC

Baby Professor Books are available at special discounts when purchased in bulk for industrial and sales-promotional use. For details contact our Special Sales Team at Speedy Publishing LLC, 40 E Main Street, Newark, Delaware 19711 USA. Telephone (888) 248-4521 Fax: (210) 519-4043.

10 9 8 7 6 * 5 4 3 2 1

Print Edition: 9781541954021
Digital Edition: 9781541957022

See the world in pictures. Build your knowledge in style.
www.speedypublishing.com

Contents

AN ILLUSTRATION OF THE
SUPERCONTINENT PANGEA

The earth didn't always look like it does today. Before there was Asia, Africa, Antarctica, Australia, Europe, and North and South America, there was Pangaea. In this book, you will learn about plate tectonics, continental drift, and how Pangaea became seven continents. Let's take a trip to the past!

Continental Drift

The surface of the earth has been changing for millions of years. Continents break apart and crash into each other. Oceans grow and shrink. Mountains form and volcanoes erupt. The earth is still changing today.

VOLCANO ERUPTION

CONTINENTAL DRIFT

Permian period
225 million years ago

PANGAEA

Triassic period
200 million years ago

LAURASIA

GONDWANA

Jurassic period
150 million years ago

Cretaceous period
65 million years ago

Present days

NORTH AMERICA

EUROPE

ASIA

AFRICA

SOUTH AMERICA

AUSTRALIA

ANTARCTICA

The continents are slowly moving across the surface of the earth. They move between 2 and 4 inches (5.08 and 10.16 centimeters) per year. In a million years, they move between 30 and 60 miles (48.28 and 96.56 kilometers). This movement is called continental drift. The theory of continental drift developed over time.

About 200 years ago, Alexander von Humboldt noticed that South America and Africa looked like they would fit together like pieces of a puzzle.

In about 1850, Antonio Snider-Pellegrini discovered that the same plant fossils could be found in North America and Europe.

ANTONIO SNIDER-PELLEGRINI

FRANK B. TAYLOR

In 1908, Frank B. Taylor theorized that mountains were formed by continents crashing into each other.

ALFRED WEGENER

Finally, in 1912, Alfred Wegener had the idea that all the continents were connected into one giant supercontinent.

Convection Currents

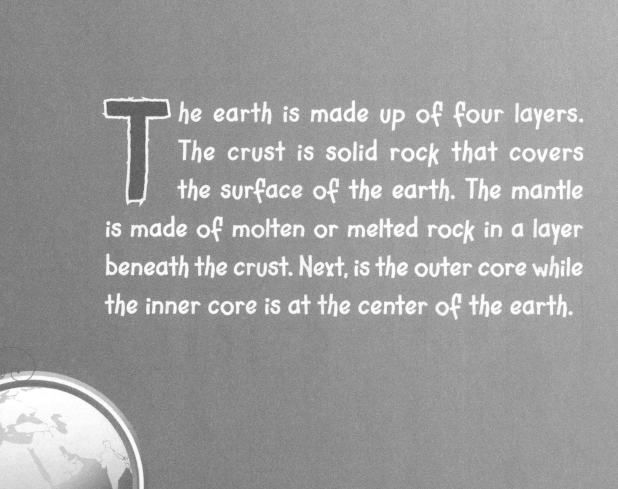

The earth is made up of four layers. The crust is solid rock that covers the surface of the earth. The mantle is made of molten or melted rock in a layer beneath the crust. Next, is the outer core while the inner core is at the center of the earth.

STRUCTURE OF THE EARTH

Crust
(8 to 40 kilometers)

Mantle
(2,900 kilometers)

Outer core
(2,250 kilometers)

Inner core
(1,300 kilometers)

LITHOSPHERE

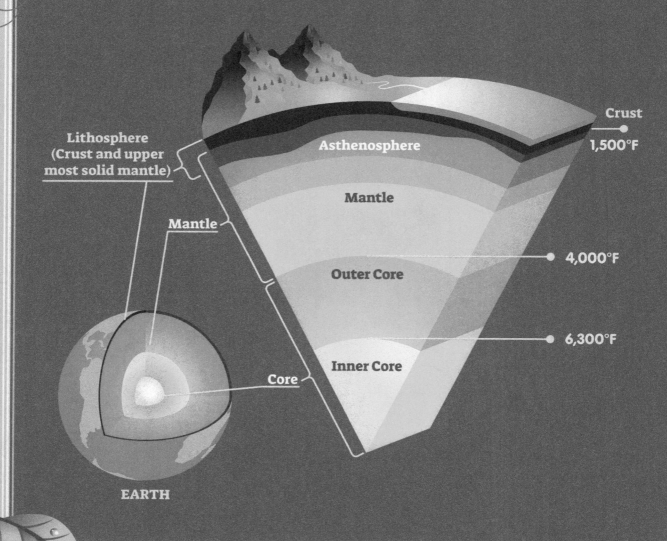

Lithosphere (Crust and upper most solid mantle)

Mantle

Core

Asthenosphere

Mantle

Outer Core

Inner Core

Crust
1,500°F

4,000°F

6,300°F

EARTH

It is believed that the inner core is somewhere around 6,300° Fahrenheit (3,482.22° Celsius)! Magma in the mantle near the outer core is heated to over 4,000° Fahrenheit (2,204.44° Celsius). The hot magma near the core rises toward the crust and starts to cool. Magma near the crust is almost 1,500° Fahrenheit (815.55° Celsius). That's the temperature of magma that erupts from volcanoes and becomes lava. As magma cools near the crust, it sinks down toward the core and gets reheated.

The swirling motion created by the heated magma rising and the cooled magma sinking is called a convection current. Convection currents happen when air and water are heated too. When water is heated in a pot, the water near the fire at the bottom of the pot boils up to the surface in the middle of the pot. The water on the surface moves from the center of the pot to the outside of the pot. Then the water sinks to the bottom and gets reheated.

Colt water sinks

Colt water sinks

Hot water rises

DIAGRAM ILLUSTRATING HOW HEAT
IS TRANSFERRED IN A BOILING POT

CONVECTION CURRENTS

Intrusion of Magma pushes the Plates away

Plates flow on the Convection currents

Oceanic Ridge

Convection currents

Plate sinks into the Subduction Zone

Trench with Subduction Zone

Lithosphere

Asthenosphere

Convection Cell

Heat slowly rises through the Mantle

Mantle

Outer Core

Inner Core

| 1216 km | 2270 km | 2885 km | |
| Inner Core | Outer Core | Mantle | |

100 km
Lithosphere

Convection currents inside the earth cause the continents to move. The continuous circular flow of magma pushes tectonic plates around. Continental drift is part of the theory of plate tectonics.

Plate
Tectonics

The earth's crust is made up of several huge chunks of rock. These pieces are called tectonic plates. Tectonic plates move in many ways.

TECTONIC PLATES

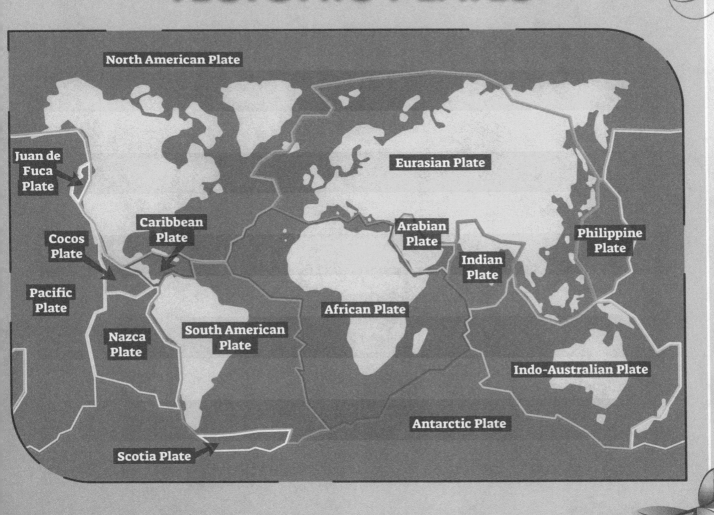

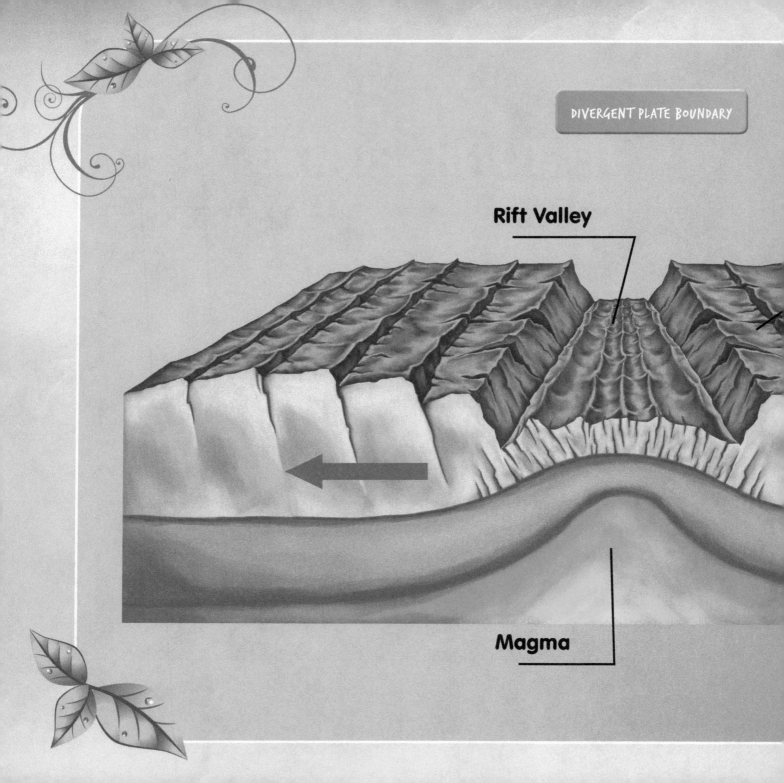

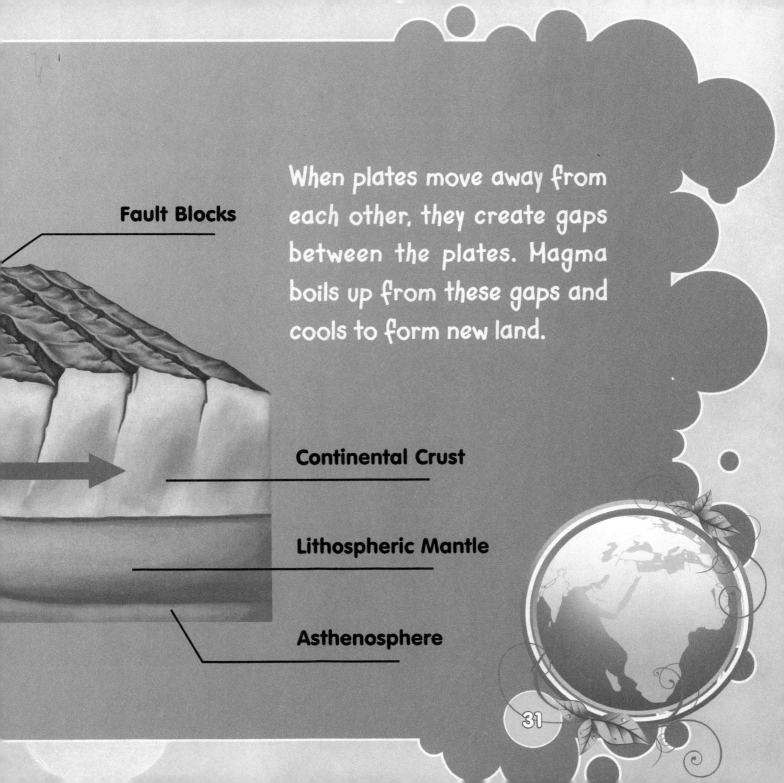

Fault Blocks

When plates move away from each other, they create gaps between the plates. Magma boils up from these gaps and cools to form new land.

Continental Crust

Lithospheric Mantle

Asthenosphere

Plates moving towards each other crash together. Sometimes one plate moves under the other and volcanoes form.

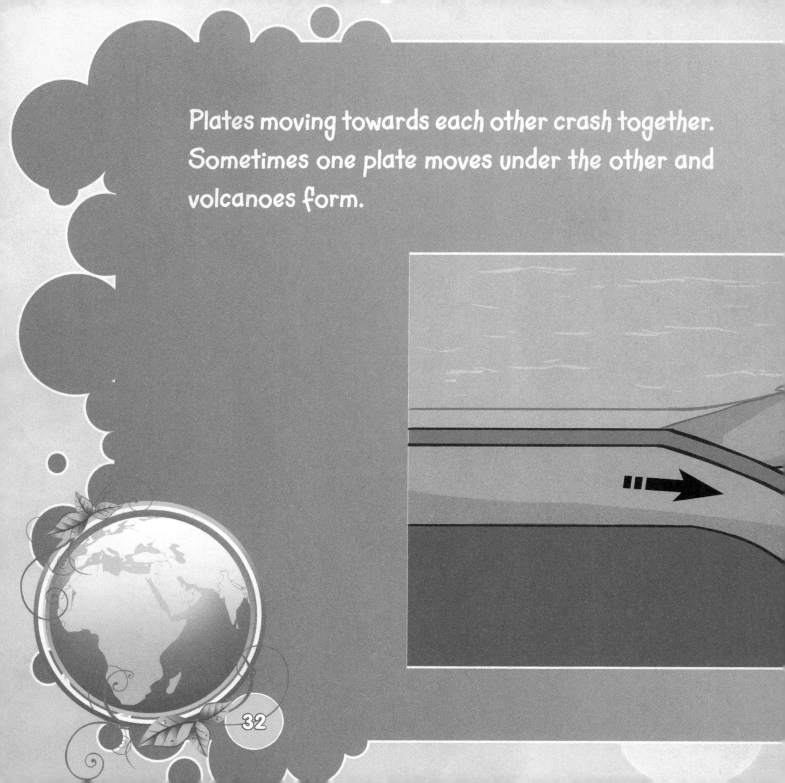

A PLATE THAT SLIPS UNDER ANOTHER CREATES VOLCANOES.

Other times, the two plates crumple together and form mountains.

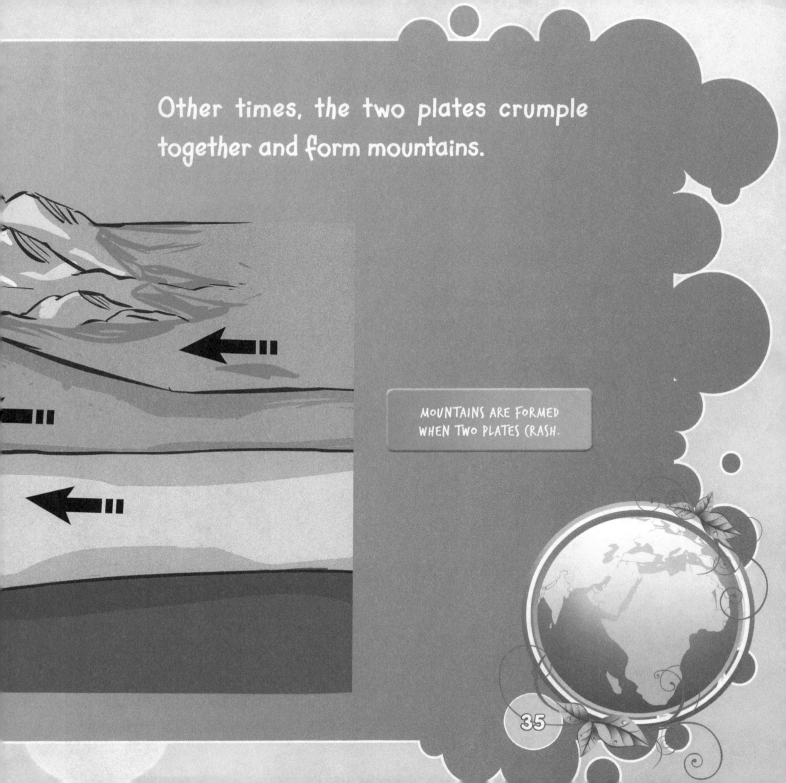

MOUNTAINS ARE FORMED WHEN TWO PLATES CRASH.

Mountains that form this way are called folded mountains. The Appalachian Mountains are folded mountains.

FOLDED MOUNTAIN FORMATION IN LADAKH, INDIA

When two plates slide past each other in opposite directions, they make fault lines.

TRANSFORM PLATE BOUNDARY

PLATE BOUNDARIES

DIVERGENT PLATE BOUNDARY

CONVERGENT PLATE BOUNDARY

TRANSFORM PLATE BOUNDARY

Oceanic Ridge

Oceanic Trench

Transform Fault

OCEAN

CRUST

MANTLE

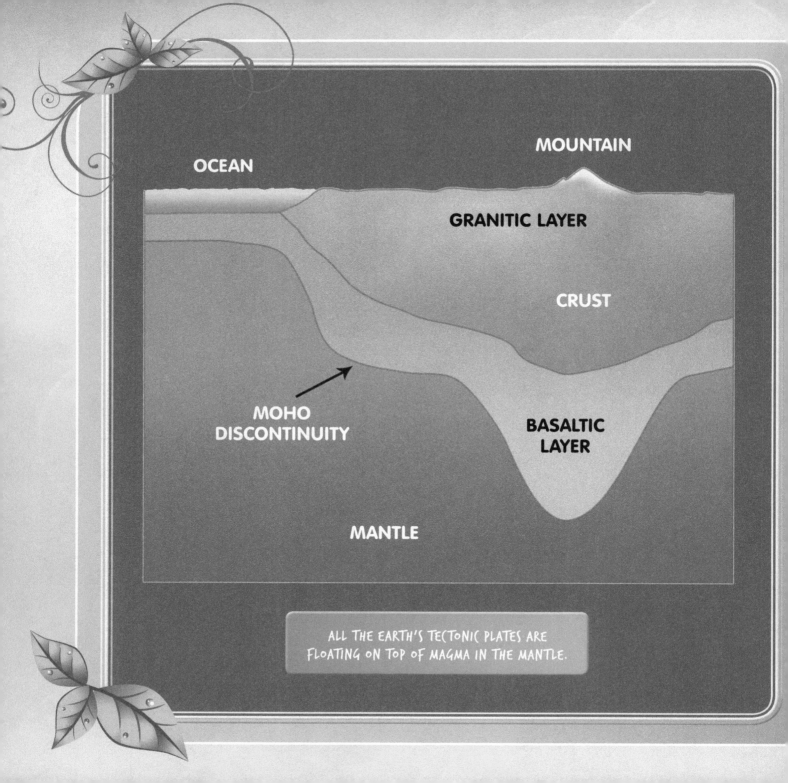

OCEAN

MOUNTAIN

GRANITIC LAYER

CRUST

MOHO
DISCONTINUITY

BASALTIC
LAYER

MANTLE

ALL THE EARTH'S TECTONIC PLATES ARE
FLOATING ON TOP OF MAGMA IN THE MANTLE.

All the earth's tectonic plates are floating on top of magma in the mantle. Plates that make up dry land are mostly granite and less dense than plates at the bottom of the ocean. This makes them float *higher* on the mantle, so they stay above the water. Tectonic plates under the ocean are mostly made of basalt. Basalt is denser than granite, so ocean plates usually slide under the plates that make up dry land.

Pangaea

Africa, Australia, Antarctica, Europe, Asia, and North and South America were once all one continent called Pangaea. The supercontinent was named Pangaea by Alfred Wegener. Pangaea means "all land". On Pangaea, North and South America made up the west coast of the continent. Europe and Asia, or Eurasia, was in the northeast. Africa was mostly in the middle. India and part of Africa made up the east coast. Australia and Antarctica were on the south end of the continent. There was only one ocean that went all the way around the world. It was called the Tethys Ocean.

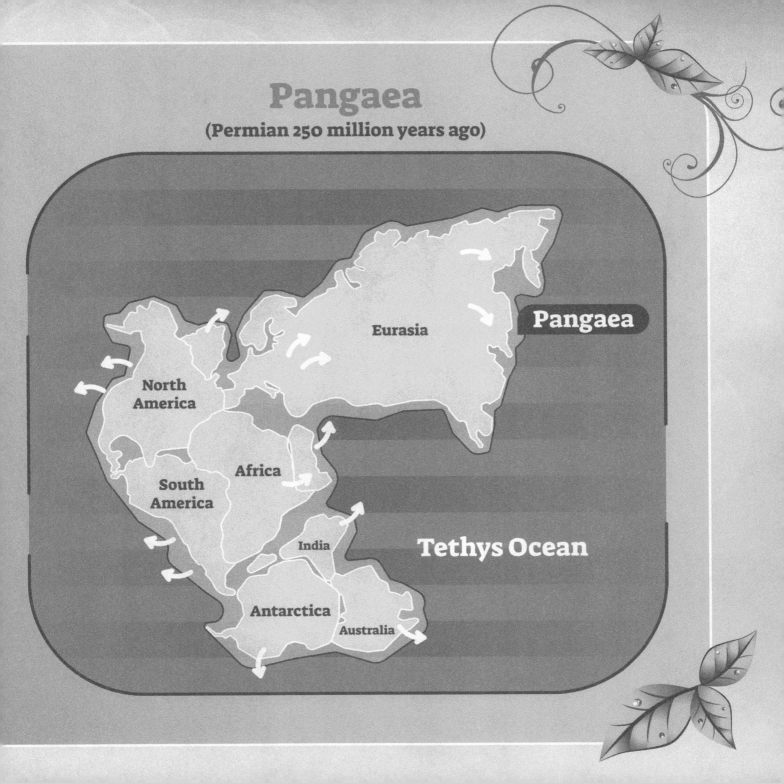

Laurasia and Gondwana

(Triassic 200 million years ago)

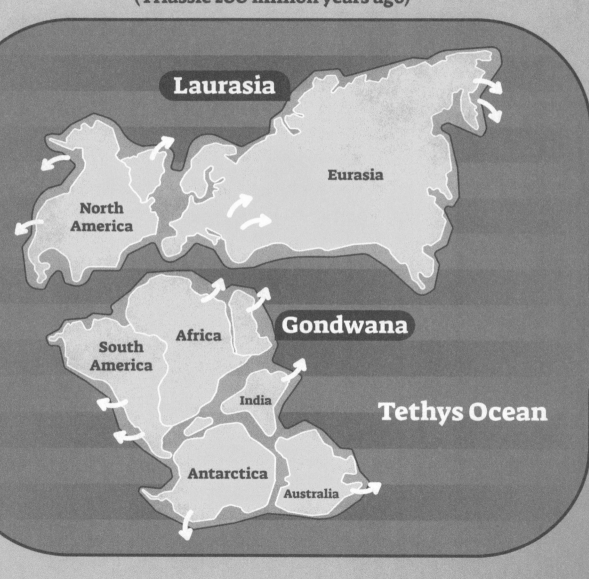

Laurasia

North America

Eurasia

Gondwana

South America

Africa

India

Tethys Ocean

Antarctica

Australia

About 225 million years ago, Pangaea started to break apart. It split apart from the middle and formed two giant continents. The northern continent was named Laurasia. The southern continent was named Gondwana. The Tethys Ocean separated them. Later, Laurasia split up to make North America and Eurasia. South America, Antarctica, Australia, India, and Africa broke away from Gondwana.

At the bottom of the ocean, the plates were moving apart, and the Mid-Atlantic Ridge formed. As magma continued to boil up, it formed new land and the continents moved further and further away from each other.

THE MID-ATLANTIC RIDGE IS SEEN IN A SPECTACULAR WAY IN ICELAND.

THE HIMALAYAN MOUNTAINS IN ASIA

As time went on, the Tethys Ocean got smaller and smaller as Africa moved closer to Eurasia. The Mediterranean Sea is all that is left of the Tethys Ocean today. India moved to the north and crashed into Eurasia. As the two plates smashed together, the Himalayan Mountains were formed. The Himalayas are getting taller every year because these plates keep pushing together.

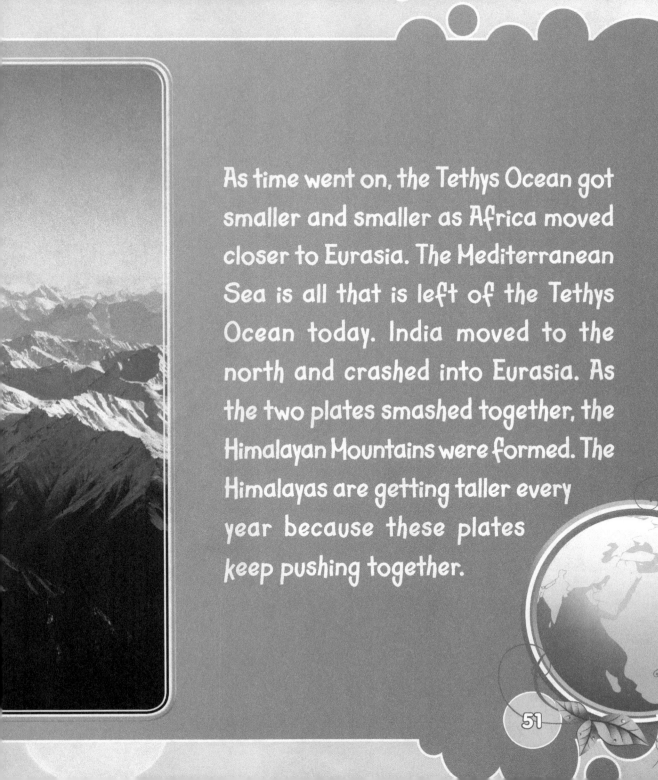

The Rocky Mountains and Andes mountains both formed as the North American and South American plates drifted into the Pacific plate. Many volcanoes and earthquakes occur where those plates touch.

A VIEW OF THE ROCKY MOUNTAINS IN PETER LOUGHEED PROVINCIAL PARK, KANANASKIS COUNTRY, ALBERTA, CANADA

ARCTIC OCEAN

GREENLAND

LABRADOR SEA

HUDSON BAY

CANADA

UNITED STATES OF AMERICA

ATLANTIC OCEAN

PACIFIC OCEAN

MEXICO

GULF OF MEXICO

BAHAMAS

CUBA

JAMAICA

HAITI

DOMINICAN REPUBLIC

PUERTO RICO

ST. KITTS AND NEVIS

ANTIGUA AND BARBUDA

GUADELOUPE

ST. LUCIA

BARBADOS

ST. VINCENT AND GRENADINES

GRENADA

TRINIDAD AND TOBAGO

BELIZE

GUATEMALA

SAN SALVADOR

HONDURAS

NICARAGUA

COSTA RICA

CARIBBEAN SEA

PANAMA

VENEZUELA

GUYANA

SURINAME

FRENCH GUIANA

COLOMBIA

ECUADOR

PERU

BRAZIL

BOLIVIA

PARAGUAY

CHILE

ARGENTINA

URUGUAY

PACIFIC OCEAN

ATLANTIC OCEAN

PANAMA CONNECTED NORTH AND SOUTH AMERICA

North America and South America are connected today, but not from crashing into each other like other continents. Volcanoes beneath the ocean formed a chain of mountains that rose above the sea. These volcanoes eventually formed Panama. This isthmus connected North and South America.

The Appalachian Mountains have been around since Pangaea first formed. They are over 300 million years old and were created when North America crashed into Africa. They have been weathered down over the years to about half the height they were when they started.

ROAN HIGHLANDS, SOUTHERN APPALACHIAN MOUNTAIN NEAR THE STATE BORDERS OF NORTH CAROLINA AND TENNESSEE

The Changing Earth

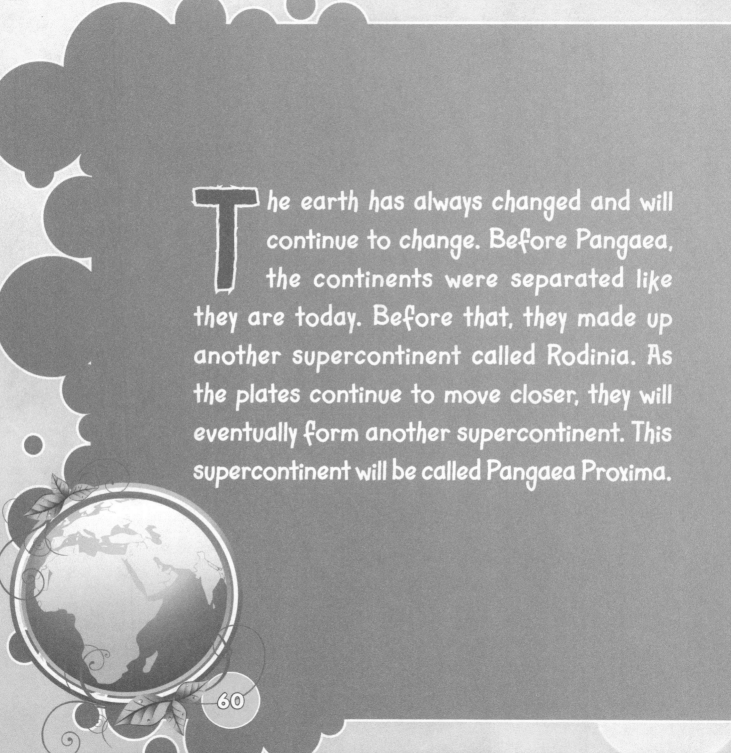

The earth has always changed and will continue to change. Before Pangaea, the continents were separated like they are today. Before that, they made up another supercontinent called Rodinia. As the plates continue to move closer, they will eventually form another supercontinent. This supercontinent will be called Pangaea Proxima.

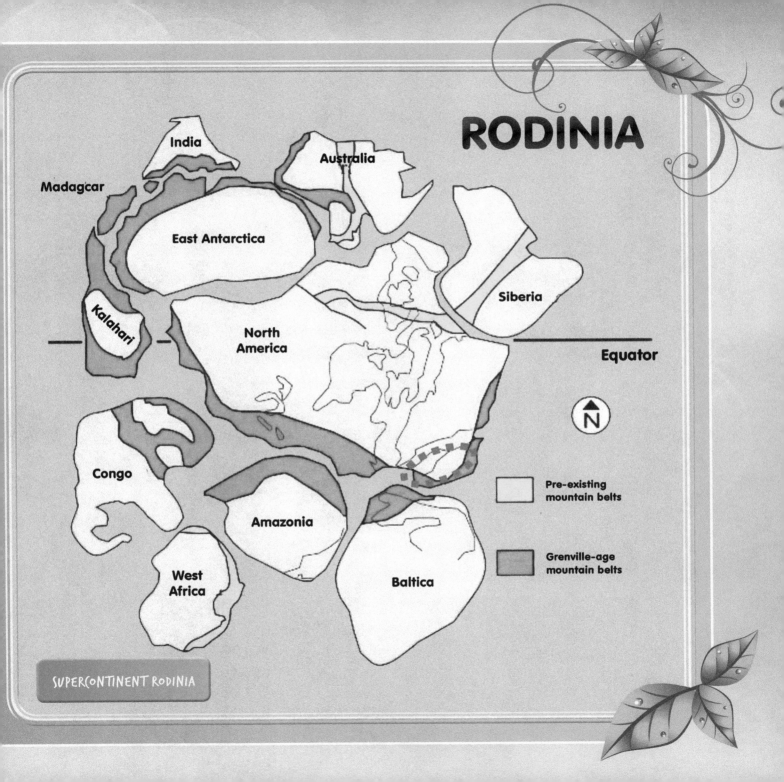

RODINIA

India

Madagcar

Australia

East Antarctica

Kalahari

Siberia

North America

Equator

N

Congo

Pre-existing
mountain belts

Amazonia

Grenville-age
mountain belts

West
Africa

Baltica

SUPERCONTINENT RODINIA

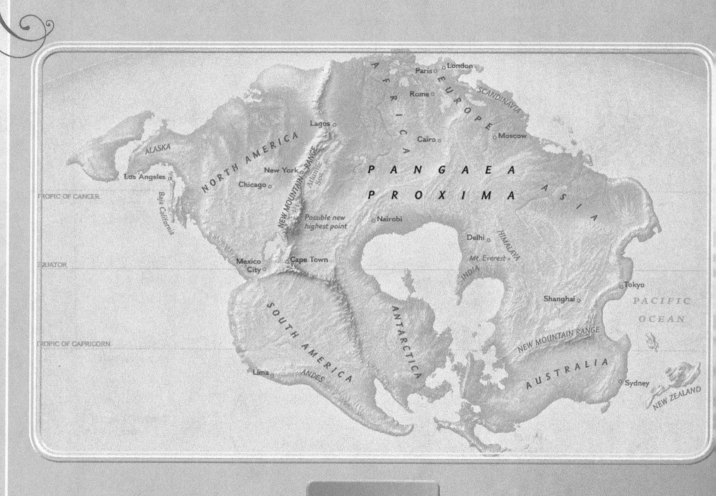

PANGAEA PROXIMA

On Pangaea Proxima, North and South America will form the west and south coasts. Africa will be north of South America and touch the arctic circle. Eurasia will be connected to Africa in the middle and form the west and south coasts. The southern tip of Eurasia will connect to the tip of South America forming a huge inland sea. Antarctica and Australia will crash together to form a giant island south of Pangaea Proxima.

Summary

The earth's continents are always moving. They only move about 2 to 4 inches (5.08 to 10.16 centimeters) each year, but that adds up over millions of years. The movement of the continents is called continental drift. Alexander von Humboldt, Antonio Snider-Pellegrini, Frank B. Taylor, and Alfred Wegener all helped to develop the theory of continental drift.

Magma near the center of the earth gets heated and rises toward the earth's crust. It cools and sinks back down where it gets reheated. As the magma gets heated and cools and gets reheated, it moves in a circle. This is called a convection current. Convection currents inside the earth are what cause the earth's tectonic plates to move.

Tectonic plates can move toward each other, away from each other, or slide past each other. Plates can move under each other and form volcanoes or press together and form mountains. When plates slide past each other, they make fault lines.

When several continents connect together, they form a supercontinent. Pangaea was a supercontinent that existed about 225 million years ago. North and South America made up the west coast. Eurasia was in the northeast. India and part of Africa made up the east coast. Australia and Antarctica were on the south end of the continent. The Tethys Ocean covered the rest of the Earth.

Pangaea broke in two and formed Laurasia and Gondwana. Laurasia broke into North America and Eurasia. Gondwana broke apart and formed the other continents that we see today. The Himalayan Mountains formed when India crashed into Eurasia. The Rocky and Andes Mountains formed when North and South America crashed into the Pacific plate. Africa moved north and connected to Eurasia.

Rodinia was a supercontinent that existed before Pangaea. The next supercontinent will be called Pangaea Proxima. No one knows for sure what the earth will look like after that, but one thing is for sure, the earth will keep changing!

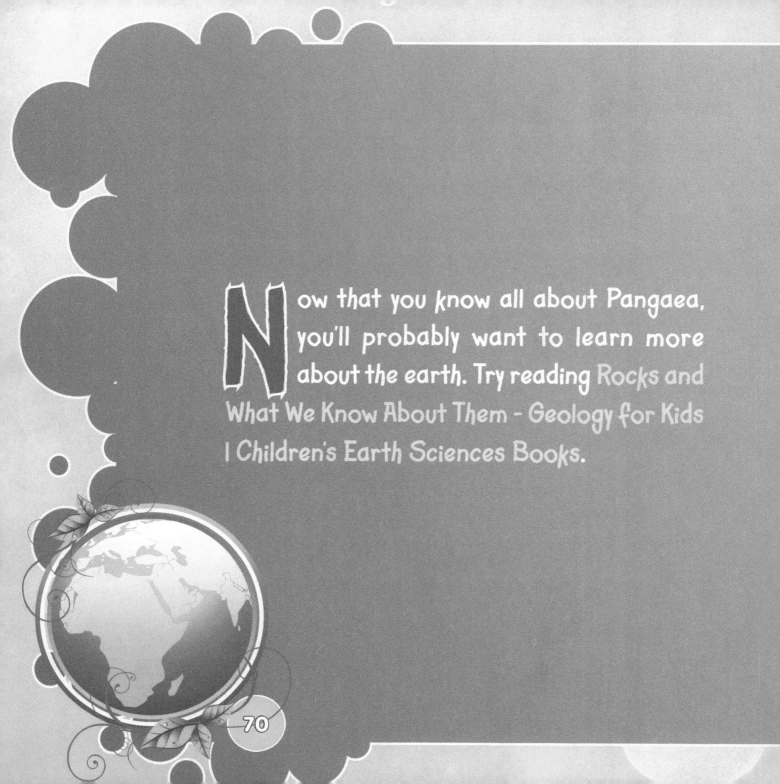

Now that you know all about Pangaea, you'll probably want to learn more about the earth. Try reading Rocks and What We Know About Them - Geology for Kids I Children's Earth Sciences Books.

CPSIA information can be obtained
at www.ICGtesting.com
Printed in the USA
LVHW060048060721
691873LV00005B/908